Jumble Box

JUMBLE BOX

Haiku and Senryu from National Haiku Writing Month

Michael Dylan Welch, *Editor*

Ron C. Moss, *Artwork*

PRESS HERE
SAMMAMISH, WASHINGTON

Press Here

22230 NE 28th Place
Sammamish, Washington
98074-6408 USA

ISBN 978-1-878798-39-8

Copyright © 2017 by Michael Dylan Welch
Artwork copyright © 2017 by Ron C. Moss

All rights revert to the authors upon publication in this book. No part of this book may be used or reproduced in any manner whatsoever without written permission from the contributor except in the case of brief quotations in reviews.

First printing, September 2017.

Design and typography by Michael Dylan Welch.
Thank you to Corine Timmer for proofreading assistance.

Poems and prose set in 13/16 and 13/20 Nyala.
Headings set in 20/24 and 24/28 Lithos Pro Black.

National Haiku Writing Month
www.nahaiwrimo.com or visit NaHaiWriMo on Facebook

Contents

Opening the Jumble Box 7

February 1: HAIKU 11
February 2: IS 21
February 3: A 31
February 4: HAND 39
February 5: BECKONING 51
February 6: A DOOR 59
February 7: HALF 65
February 8: OPENED 73
February 9: A MIRROR 81
February 10: WIPED 89
February 11: CLEAN 95
February 12: IT 103
February 13: IS 111
February 14: A WAY OF 117
February 15: RETURNING TO 125
February 16: NATURE 133
February 17: MOON 139
February 18: NATURE 147

February 19: CHERRY BLOSSOM 153
February 20: NATURE 163
February 21: FALLING. 169
February 22: LEAF 175
February 23: NATURE 183
February 24: IN SHORT 189
February 25: TO. 197
February 26: OUR 205
February 27: BUDDHA. 213
February 28: NATURE 223

Next Steps with Haiku 231
Contributing Poets. 237

Opening the Jumble Box

ONE OF MY FAVORITE QUOTATIONS about haiku is by R. H. Blyth: "Haiku is a hand beckoning, a door half-opened, a mirror wiped clean. It is a way of returning to nature, to our moon nature, our cherry blossom nature, our falling leaf nature, in short, to our Buddha nature." This observation reminds us that haiku points to a source. It inspired my daily writing prompts for the seventh episode of the annual celebration known as National Haiku Writing Month, or NaHaiWriMo, held in February of 2017. Beginning and experienced haiku poets from around the world responded to these prompts with thousands of haiku and senryu (the index includes poet locations to tell you where they're from). I chose this book's 324 poems, by exactly 100 poets, for their individual resonance and poetic quality, and for their creative ways in responding to the prompts. Look for celebrated similarity among some poems, yet also diversity and variety in others, all contributing to an energetic jumble box of poets and poetry.

National Haiku Writing Month first took place in 2011 with the goal to write at least one haiku a day for each day of February, the year's shortest month for the world's shortest genre of poetry.

Each year, hundreds of participants share their haiku and senryu on the NaHaiWriMo page on Facebook, and I'm grateful to this active community for producing the poems in this anthology. In a way, this book is twenty-eight smaller books, with chapters for each day of February offering sets of poems themed to match each daily prompt. Perhaps read just one chapter a day, taking up to an entire month to read this book. And while you're at it, try writing a new haiku of your own in response to the prompt for each day. Please also join us for the next National Haiku Writing Month celebration, held every February.

The following poems emerged as some of the best from many thousands written for NaHaiWriMo in 2017. I shared a short list of about 400 selections with Tasmanian artist Ron C. Moss, who chose one poem for each day of the month. In response, he created twenty-eight original haiga—a painting for each poem he selected, with the poem added in calligraphy. He also created the cover art, and suggested the book's title, from a poem by Greg Longenecker. Surely the many ways we write haiku are like a jumble box—and as with a box of chocolates, you never know what you'll discover. Special thanks to Ron for his artwork, and to each poet who participated in NaHaiWriMo. May their moments of poetic inspiration now be yours as a way of returning to yourself and what matters in the world around you.

Indeed, through each one of this book's poems I hope we can return to nature—our moon nature, our cherry blossom nature, our falling leaf nature—for it is nature and its seasonal unfoldings that provide much of haiku's inspiration. Likewise, human nature inspires haiku's more humorous or satirical cousin, senryu. I will leave up to each individual reader to contemplate whether this poetry also returns us to our Buddha nature, but I trust that it at least returns us to the essences of deeply felt personal experience, to the joy of creativity with language, and to a heightened appreciation for our varied and wonderful world.

Michael Dylan Welch
National Haiku Writing Month Founder

February 1

haiku (a poem about haiku)

cricket in the grass
is there a haiku
just for you

— Nikolay Penchev

jumble box
all my unfinished
haiku

Greg Longenecker

another chance
to know the ordinary
winter meadow

Anne Burgevin

first spring birds
the haiku group spreads
through the park

Tore Sverredal

scrap of paper
a haiku fades
in the sun

Barbara Strang

his death haiku
tied to the kite string—
wild grasses

Michael Dylan Welch

writing haiku

the wind insists

I start over

John Hawk

shooting star

the old poet writes

her death haiku

Susan E. Buffington

new moon

my niece writes

her first haiku

Gergana Yaninska

a tiny poem

for a tiny moment:

hummingbird wings

    Erica Olson

an aha moment

stumbling on a step

that isn't there

    Shrikaanth Krishnamurthy

crowded subway—

the heat and the smell

and a book of haiku

    Rahmatou Sangotte

wild grasses—

desperately looking

for the lost haiku

    Vincent Hoarau

contemplating

how to write haiku

blustery day

    James Rodriguez

first light—

the haiku I wrote

better in my dream

    Shelley Krause

pale winter sky—

an unfinished haiku

in my draft folder

    Paul David Mena

cricket in the grass

is there a haiku

just for you

    Nikolay Penchev

FEBRUARY 2

is

winter wind
the last leaf now
on top of the pile

— Stella Pierides

morning sun

time to breathe

and just be

    Deborah P Kolodji

a light changes

this rain that could be

snow

    Angie Werren

the who

behind who I am . . .

cloudless sky

    Michele L. Harvey

first thunderclap the echoes of startled birds

Sandi Pray

a skip in the step of the child—lolly shop

Belinda Broughton

winter sunshine the robin outsings me

Caroline Skanne

meditation—

finding proof of god

in a hummingbird

    Sara Winteridge

full moon

she almost scratches

her mosquito bites

    Helene Jäderberg

in the center

of the morning glory . . .

everything

    Terri L. French

a bit of down stuck

to the egg in an aerie—

the encircling stars

Linda Papanicolaou

lazy breeze

the magician

and the unshuffled deck

Cameron Mount

wind in the branches

weather forecast

with sign language

Viktoriya Marinova

park bench

the way the ducks quack

like I'm not there

    Christine L. Villa

becoming an echo . . .

a pine needle slips

into a broken nest

    Kathy Uyen Nguyen

the reassurance

of a friendly touch . . .

snow-dusted trees

Marietta McGregor

soft tears again

for this unknown grief—

the silhouettes of crows

Joanna Paterson

meditation

pink glow of dawn

behind the pines

Barbara Kaufmann

refugees

left with nothing

but their lives

Alison Williams

day moon I learn to just be

Samar Ghose

winter wind

the last leaf now

on top of the pile

Stella Pierides

FEBRUARY 3

a

almost free
 the anchor
holding the child's kite

— Robert Kingston

A is for apple—

a winter day spent

teaching the toddler

      Carole MacRury

winter moon

the A-bomb dome

casting a shadow

      Johnny Baranski

not on

anybody's A-list

dandelion blooms

Deborah P Kolodji

opera première

the breathless silence

after the tuning

Tore Sverredal

the old woman

touching the letters

of a tombstone

Paul David Mena

silent wind chime

the way a single glance

leaves a mark

Anitha Varma

always there not there like the schwa in father my father

Samar Ghose

Amadeus . . .

a feather lifts and spirals

just out of reach

Sheila Windsor

winter sunlight a whisper of dove wings

Barbara Kaufmann

Azaleas

the cat sleeps under

a cloud of flowers

Karla Decker

appaloosa sky

a herd of clouds

grazing

Michael Henry Lee

Aberystwyth

via Abergavenny

mist-shrouded mountains

Rachel Green

almost free

the anchor

holding the child's kite

Robert Kingston

FEBRUARY 4
hand

origami...
the boat in the ocean
in her hand

— Sheila Windsor

potter's wheel

the way the clay

shapes her hands

Terri L. French

stacks of paper

several hands high . . .

where does it all belong?

Robert T. Franson

a guilty verdict

handed down . . .

freezing rain

Johnny Baranski

tiny hand—

such a grasp

on my heart

Patty Hardin

handing over

the keys to the car—

dementia diagnosis

Amy Losak

touched by light . . .

my mother's hands

in the old photograph

Samar Ghose

first steps

her little hand

in mine

Tore Sverredal

silver dollar in my hand,

Grandpa and I

walk to town

Marilyn Deavers

the preteen's hand
no longer reaches for mine
mockingbird calls

    Cameron Mount

first date
his sweaty hand
reaches for mine

    Barbara Kaufmann

on the hands
of the widower . . .
mismatched mittens

    Carole MacRury

his fingers

around my finger . . .

delicate sun

    John Hawk

pale winter sky—

the honor student who never

raises his hand

    Paul David Mena

snow falling

onto the old fishing dock . . .

her hand in mine

    Michael Dylan Welch

stringing barbwire

the winter wind

in my hands

Paul Wruck

new flux of refugees

hand to hand

passing welcome bags

Carmen Sterba

First spring rain

collecting it

in the palm of his hand

Iocasta Huppen

slow dancing

on a warm afternoon

his hand and the gnats

Peggy Hale Bilbro

ancient winter stars—
the archivist's hands sheathed
in white cotton gloves

    Linda Papanicolaou

unsung . . .
the hand behind
the selfie

    Ajaya Mahala

birthday party
the clown's white gloves
speckled with glitter

    Ron C. Moss

fading light her hand at the door waving

    Rosemary Nissen-Wade

in this space

where solitude and i dwell

my folded hands

    Gillena Cox

origami . . .

the boat in the ocean

in her hand

    Sheila Windsor

February 5

beckoning

heat wave—
a blossom beckons
to the bee

— Carole MacRury

this deafness—

she follows the beckoning hand

into the crowded bar

Barbara Strang

ladies of the evening

waving as if they

knew me

Michael Henry Lee

mountain cave

suddenly a snow leopard

in moonlight

Ron C. Moss

that gap in the hedge

still beckoning explorers—

the old neighborhood

Shelley Krause

morning snow—

i share my takeout

breakfast

Mike Duffy

Valentine's Day

beckoning for a cigarette

the homeless woman

Line Jolyot

virgin snow I resist

Johannes S. H. Bjerg

day moon—

a winter thaw pulls me out

of solitude

Barbara Kaufmann

winter drizzle—

the mattress sale sign spinner

takes a break

Michael Dylan Welch

hospice window

the roar of a spring tide

receding

Sheila Windsor

come here come here come here unidentified birdsong

Cameron Mount

heat wave—

a blossom beckons

to the bee

Carole MacRury

FEBRUARY 6
a door

paw scratches
on my screen door...
first day of spring

Christine L. Villa

snow-covered hills

the sound of a radio

from the open barn door

Paul Wruck

hospital doors

the comings and goings

of a winter's day

Robert Kingston

at dusk

on the door to my motel

. . . mating moths

    Carole MacRury

moonless night—

rusted hinges

on the slaughterhouse door

    Michael Dylan Welch

trashed doll's house

the doors all open

for the field mice

    Ron C. Moss

starling's song

a door ajar

at sunset

Marina Bellini

paw scratches

on my screen door . . .

first day of spring

Christine L. Villa

February 7

half

night lamp—
he tells me only
half the truth

—Sanjuktaa Asopa

half moon

a lonely kitten on

the doorstep

Vibeke Laier

another year . . .

only one of us

on our favourite walk

Grace Galton

half hearted . . .

the old poet on

Valentine's Day

      Susan E. Buffington

flash flood only half the sign
~~⌐ PRONE TO ⌐~~

      Samar Ghose

spring warmth

my brother and I split

a popsicle

      Michele L. Harvey

memories

of our honeymoon

coconut husks

John Hawk

your side of the bed—

the space we hold

for each other

Dawn Apanius

Windy day

an empty pot makes half circles

on the terrace

Iocasta Huppen

even half asleep

we know the other is there—

the moon behind clouds

Shelley Krause

suggested edits

cut my enjoyment by half

—acceptance letter

Eric Lohman

chocolate hard from the fridge can't cut you half what a pity

Rosemary Nissen-Wade

half way through

the board meeting

skylight rain

    Sheila Windsor

night lamp—

he tells me only

half the truth

    Sanjuktaa Asopa

February 8

opened

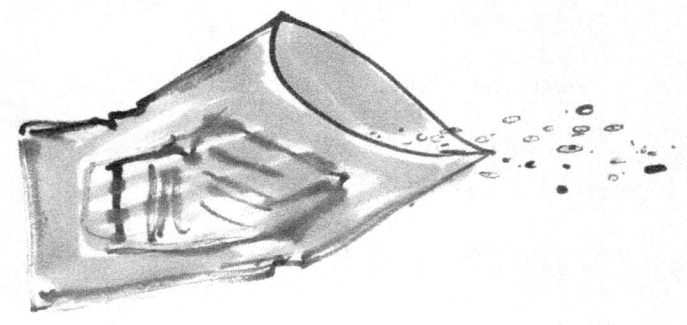

Seed pack opened—
how my garden
will be this year

— Dawn Apanius

a hand is

beckoning—

the half-opened door

    Barbara Strang

opened door

a white lilac scent

comes my way

    Marie-Alice Maire

old barn door

open just enough

for time to pass

Sandi Pray

sultry evening

neighbours' baby

in full voice

Rowena McGregor

lingering dream

sun's warmth orange

on my lids

Anitha Varma

that moment

when forgiveness is granted . . .

wind-rippled grass

    Michele L. Harvey

from down the block

he hears the can

of opened tuna

    Michael Henry Lee

the window opened

a little bird wants to share

my lunch

    Helene Jäderberg

opened can—

the expensive meat

the cat won't eat

    Bill Waters

mountain chalet—

the coolness at my feet

in front of the fridge

    Michael Dylan Welch

winter fog—

a newly opened

line of credit

    Paul David Mena

still unopened

the boxes we moved

from her last room

Kathabela Wilson

late winter

the sky opens up

to the stars

Tore Sverredal

seed pack opened—

how my garden

will be this year

Dawn Apanius

FEBRUARY 9
a mirror

night falls
on the mirror
leaving me alone

—Michael A. Moore

midwinter

the face in the mirror

avoids eye contact

Johannes S. H. Bjerg

cataract surgery—

the wrinkles

I never knew I had

Pamela Cooper

bathing suit season

someone else's thighs

in the dressing room mirror

Terri L. French

on the bathroom mirror

"It's over," scrawled

in lipstick

Johnny Baranski

probing deeper

the dentist moves

his mirror

Robert Kingston

funhouse mirrors

she finds one with the right

reflection

    Helene Jäderberg

snow on the windowsill

my Mommy's hair

on the mirror

    Gergana Yaninska

during chemo,

in each morning's mirror

my newborn head

    Penny Harter

window shopping glimpses of my mother

Sara Winteridge

I remember her now—

a face in this old silvered

mirror

Angie Werren

night falls

on the mirror

leaving me alone

Michael A. Moore

February 10

wiped

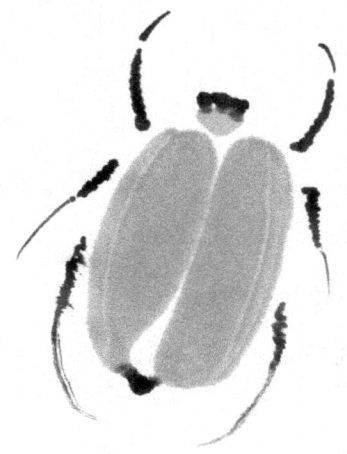

what's left
of the june bug
sunset drive

— John Hawk

the counter wiped

and coffee brewing . . .

I whistle a tune

Bill Waters

traffic jam—

the unchanging rhythm

of windshield wipers

Ida Freilinger

my steps fill with snow

all trace of my passing

wiped out by the wind

Shelley Krause

summer heat . . .
the table wiped clean
at the morgue

    Michael Dylan Welch

to and fro
across the rainbow
car wipers

    Sanjuktaa Asopa

what's left
of the june bug
sunset drive

    John Hawk

FEBRUARY 11
clean

among the crocus
and melting snow
a bare bone

—Peggy Hale Bilbro

after their deaths

I lose them again, cleaning

out my parent's home

Penny Harter

words I regret

scrubbing my sink

over and over

Christine L. Villa

washing curtains—
all the windows draped
in sky

    Sanjuktaa Asopa

school girls
clean the chalk erasers
on one another

    Marilyn Ashbaugh

chafing sails . . .
he finally comes clean
about the redhead

    Pris Campbell

clean as a whistle—

and then I see

the whistle

Paul David Mena

clean street

a boy is cycling

with big mirrors

Nikolay Penchev

stage set

the janitors last sweep

before lights out

Robert Kingston

snowmelt

little sparrow bathes

in the big blue sky

Pat Nelson

clean window

my reflection

vanishes

Ardelle Ray

the food bank

shelves picked clean

snow moon

Johnny Baranski

among the crocus

and melting snow

a bare bone

Peggy Hale Bilbro

FEBRUARY 12
it

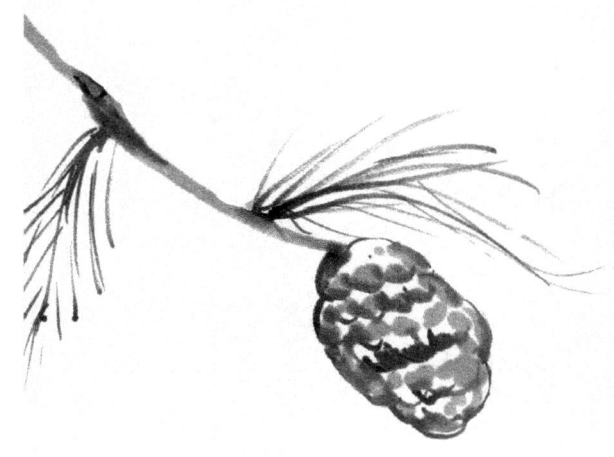

Snow on the pine
she writes a new haiku
on a pink post-it

— Helene Jäderberg

whispers . . .

the redhead is the girl

who has it

    Pris Campbell

nice, but what is it?

a viewer's head tilts sideways

at the spring art fair

    Linda Papanicolaou

no surprise

that it's a surprise . . .

sixtieth year

    Michele L. Harvey

it takes a village—

the peaceful song

of chirping birds

    Deborah B. Shepherd

clouds—

the urge

to try it

    Rahmatou Sangotte

the pale right wing

luminous and torn,

it rests a while

Mary Kendall

five years old

yet how she plays it . . .

spring rain

Sheila Windsor

it freezes

on the night wind—

wolf moon

Maggie James

knowing it,

not knowing it . . .

winter sparrow

Sanjuktaa Asopa

winter moon

for a brief moment

it stops howling

Tore Sverredal

snow on the pine

she writes a new haiku

on a pink post-it

Helene Jäderberg

FEBRUARY 13

is

a dozen roses—
what is and isn't
a valentine

— Paul David Mena

footsteps

through the fog—

is it you?

Carole MacRury

frosty morning—

it is spring

more or less

Johnny Baranski

ice chunks

drift in the river . . .

spring is sprung

Randall Herman

there's a time

for everything—

melting snow

    Stella Pierides

it is what it is

I tell myself, deciphering

the wind

    Penny Harter

scarlet begonias . . .

my mother is

still in the garden

    Devin Harrison

Is it just me?

the scent of

Aleppo soap

Corine Timmer

grassy field

vibrant with

wind's isness

Hansha Teki

a dozen roses—

what is and isn't

a valentine

Paul David Mena

FEBRUARY 14
a way of

tea brewing...
the way the moon fills
the pause of cicadas

—Kathy Uyen Nguyen

blossom rain . . .

the way she laughs

at all my jokes

John Hawk

sunlight

the way a mother smiles

at her newborn

Barbara Kaufmann

mourning doves—

a way of knowing you

are here

    Angie Werren

midwinter phone call—

the way the space between us

falls away

    Shelley Krause

midwinter thaw—

the scarecrow points the way

with a shriveled radish

    Michael Dylan Welch

nature has a way of

forced remembrance

cardinal against snow

    Anne Larbes DeLorean

losing it

the way finds me—

woodland hike

    Penny Harter

the woodcarver

takes down with care

his father's tools

    Ron C. Moss

in the way

of the heron

I walk the tidepool

    Carole MacRury

the way—

the circle he paces

at the home

    Roy Kindelberger

tea brewing . . .

the way the moon fills

the pause of cicadas

    Kathy Uyen Nguyen

February 15

returning to

moon overhead
I return
to my old home

— Ajaya Mahala

dried bouquet

her hand returns

to her cheek

Susan Murata

home

the blue trout we've cooked

Valentine's Day

Line Jolyot

finding pennies

in melted snow . . .

I feel young again

    Pamela Cooper

back in the chair

my tongue explores

a new crater

    Sheila Windsor

return to sender

unexpected spring showers

wash away the snow

    Ardelle Ray

turning around

to see the cherry blossoms

once again

Michael A. Moore

old neighborhood—

the climbing tree

beyond my reach

Carole MacRury

a yawn

and a stretch

. . . returning to now

Bill Waters

returning home
I exchange Mt. Fuji
for Mt. Rainier

Carmen Sterba

frog spawn
for a little while
I am nine again

Grace Galton

wild geese
returning
the compliment

Michael Henry Lee

City of her childhood
queuing in the rain
for pretzels

    Iocasta Huppen

my old bomber jacket
I slip back into
"yes dear"

    Samar Ghose

moon overhead
I return
to my old home

    Ajaya Mahala

February 16

nature

desert willow
not yet spring
for you

—Ardelle Ray

pastel twilight
my footsteps fill the sky
with finches

Sandi Pray

the last patch of snow
on the mossy lawn . . .
a call from home

Michael Dylan Welch

almost spring and yet
stems of the friendship plant
not yet pink

Kathabela Wilson

sunbirds flit

in and out of sun beams

porch swing

    Anitha Varma

my path to joy

swallows dipping in the sky

never a straight line

    Symanntha Renn

desert willow

not yet spring

for you

    Ardelle Ray

February 17

moon

morning traffic
a waning moon
for company

— Marina Bellini

balmy night

my spirit yields to

its moon nature

      Hansha Teki

spring dawn—

almost no one sees

the prairie moon rising

      Mike Duffy

open window

tonight the moon speaks

only to me

    Allal Taleb

hunger moon . . .

the old hippie

tunes his guitar

    Robert T. Franson

blue moon—

how white

the picket fence

    Pamela Cooper

prairie grasses

shimmering

buffalo moon

Erica Olson

pay day—

a waning

gibbous moon

Paul David Mena

a coyote wanders

the cul-de-sac

vanishing moon

John Hawk

day moon

on spring ice

a lone goose

Dawn Apanius

terrorist warning . . .

the moon rises

undeterred

Ajaya Mahala

morning traffic

a waning moon

for company

Marina Bellini

February 18

nature (in another season)

birds of paradise
the bright blue tongue
of a giraffe

—Kathabela Wilson

first truly warm day—

big sister counting

the baby's toes

Shelley Krause

a bumblebee drones

from flower to flower

slow news day

Alison Williams

quiet evening

awaiting the head frog

to assemble a chorus

Carmen Sterba

leaf piles

where are all

the children?

    Cameron Mount

hoar frost

the drive home

from her lover

    Patsy Turner

birds of paradise

the bright blue tongue

of a giraffe

    Kathabela Wilson

FEBRUARY 19
cherry blossom

winter morning
 on the teapot
  cherry blossoms

— Rahmatou Sangotte

falling in love

for the first time

cherry blossom rain

    Michael Henry Lee

spring rain

pouring down

cherry blossoms

    Mike Duffy

cherry blossoms
a girl puts on
her first lipstick

    Nikolay Penchev

cherry blossoms . . .
even the toddler's tantrums
short-lived

    Kathy Uyen Nguyen

all day
the wind wanders—
cherry blossoms

    Maggie James

walking among

cherry blossoms

the blind couple

John Hawk

a string of buoys

marks the empty swim area . . .

drifting blossoms

Michael Dylan Welch

the pinkness

of my baby's fingers . . .

cherry blossoms

Anitha Varma

under my dead father's tree cherry blossoms

Pris Campbell

deserted house

only

the cherry blossoms

Marina Bellini

sakura

just what the goat

wanted for breakfast

Patsy Turner

Flight of skylarks—

prayers in the temple

turn into cherry blossoms

Virginia Popescu

cherry blossom—

I love myself

a little bit better

Nink Nonk

cherry blossoms

fill the gutters

too soon, too soon

Cameron Mount

winter morning—

on the teapot

cherry blossoms

Rahmatou Sangotte

FEBRUARY 20

nature (seasonal or unique to where you live)

tell me
how the sky
loves the stars

— Kathi Wright

red buds

always the first to know

it's spring

    Michael Henry Lee

quake anniversary

a lone spoonbill

stalks the mudflats

    Barbara Strang

Only the snow

sitting on the bench—

deserted street

    Virginia Popescu

lakeshore bonfire—

the youth choir amplified

from the Christmas ship

    Michael Dylan Welch

tell me

how the sky

loves the stars

    Kathi Wright

FEBRUARY 21
falling

falling in love
with the red hydrant:
the nosy dog
— Bill Waters

as if the stars

weren't enough . . .

falling in love

    Michele L. Harvey

reason enough to talk to a stranger falling blossoms

    Shrikaanth Krishnamurthy

finding the low points

on every branch

morning dew

    Robert Kingston

falling apart

the construction worker's

packed lunch

Stella Pierides

first rain

washing winter

from the window

Karla Decker

a falling feather lands in my path I remember you

Rosemary Nissen-Wade

first flakes

how gently you settle

on my mind

    Grace Galton

falling snow—

even the woodpecker's day

fills up with quiet

    Shelley Krause

falling in love

with the red hydrant:

the nosy dog

    Bill Waters

FEBRUARY 22
leaf

gunnera—
 a scarlet maple leaf
  deep within

　—Barbara Strang

as if there were

some fantastic ending

leaf swirl

Steve Smolak

dripping icicle . . .

a frozen leaf

extends it an inch

Paul Wruck

wandering leaf

the places I've gone

in dreams

Kathy Uyen Nguyen

how much rain

you can hold . . .

curled autumn leaf

Sanjuktaa Asopa

all at once

the crows fly off

leafless tree

John Hawk

crispy leaf

floats downstream . . .

daytime campfire

Randall Herman

leafing out . . .

baby's first step

becomes his second

Michele L. Harvey

falling leaves—

the day a tree branch broke

beneath my feet

Roy Kindelberger

always too soon

the change from leaf blower

to snow blower

    Paul David Mena

gunnera—

a scarlet maple leaf

deep within

    Barbara Strang

FEBRUARY 23

nature (human nature)

choosing
what to believe —
dead nettle

— Sara Winteridge

punt passing

a new batch of tourists

stares at the ducks

Barbara Strang

peacock feathers one selfie after another

Christine L. Villa

covering up

vomit on the museum floor

hardwood sawdust

Joseph Connolly

day-dreaming

making up my own

fake news

Pat Nelson

road rage

wasps go inside

the open door

Ron C. Moss

before I weigh myself

on the bathroom scale

shaving

Michael Dylan Welch

choosing

what to believe—

dead nettle

Sara Winteridge

FEBRUARY 24

in short (minimal)

beach day puddled ice cream

—Pris Campbell

s NO w

Sara Winteridge

salt flat sky

John Hawk

coldark

Sheila Windsor

bells

all day

snow

  Karla Decker

spring

watch

movement

  Robert Kingston

for one

show only

mayfly

  Johnny Baranski

rusty hinge—me too, me too

Cameron Mount

dreamcatcher those that get away

Anitha Varma

twilight cue the cricket chorus

Grace Galton

first frost

waiting hearse

   Michele L. Harvey

fog

lifting

shadows

   Pamela Cooper

court

room

just

ice

   Michael Dylan Welch

cold comfort—

spending February

in shorts

Eric Lohman

ants—

coming

or going?

Ajaya Mahala

beach day puddled ice cream

Pris Campbell

FEBRUARY 25

to

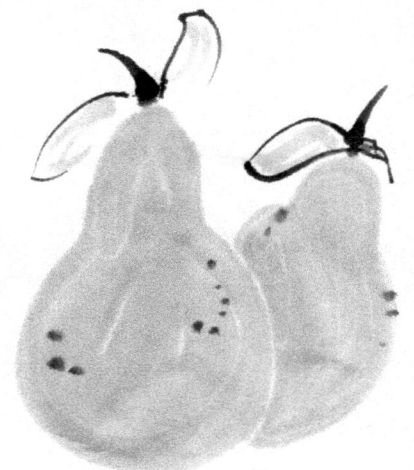

to-do list
  pears
  ripen

—Patsy Turner

to do . . .

erase all

to-do's

Robert T. Franson

to be or not to be

that parent

in the crowd

Paul David Mena

storm watch

treetops whisper

branch to branch

    Terri L. French

level crossing . . .

roadside daisies nodding

to the wind

    Jayashree Maniyil

along the road,

listening to the bird song

among the raindrops

    Nicole Pottier

to speak

in stars

would be

to know

the dark

    Kathi Wright

dew

leaf

to

leaf

silence

    Shrikaanth Krishnamurthy

as if to say

no, not yet

late-season snow

Michele L. Harvey

to and fro . . .

the nest builders

choosing names

Sara Winteridge

summer wind

during the solemn talk

she needs to sneeze

Helene Jäderberg

cool summer fog

just before dawn

chocolate donettes to go

    Anne Larbes DeLorean

out to lunch

the waitress smiles

at the daffodils

    Robert Kingston

to-do list

pear

ripens

    Patsy Turner

February 26

our

our time together
short but sweet
prison yard snow

—Johnny Baranski

our walk, among

daffodils and magnolia blossoms

winter ends

Steve Smolak

winter's end

things that were ours

now yours or mine

Alison Williams

in the living room
dancing with our mother
father

Joseph Connolly

spring frost
the awkwardness
of our first kiss

John Hawk

dappled shade our first walk together

Christine L. Villa

soft mantras

our little cat falls into

her last dream

        Helene Jäderberg

our blanket

apparently

is just yours

        Michael Dylan Welch

at the protest site—

tearing down a sign reading

"this land is our land"

        Paul David Mena

our wild stories

around the campfire

crackle with the flames

    Ron C. Moss

our time together

short but sweet

prison yard snow

    Johnny Baranski

FEBRUARY 27
Buddha

a snowy path...
candles lead to
Buddha

— Corine Timmer

spring greening

the stone buddha's smile

remains unchanged

    Alison Williams

summer afternoon—

the frogs and i

meditating

    Mike Duffy

bedeviling me

out of my buddha mind

one lone fly

Michele L. Harvey

Buddha under snow—

for him too

seasons move on

Iocasta Huppen

on the road

hoping not

to meet the Buddha

Terri L. French

hazardous load

dashboard Buddha

leads the way

John Hawk

after the rain

camellia blossoms underfoot—

Buddha path

Devin Harrison

who knows what evil

lurks in the hearts of men?

the Buddha knows

Johnny Baranski

garden party . . .

the old poet wears

her Buddha smile

    Susan E. Buffington

after the meal

the belly of the Buddha

is just how I feel

    Scott Dickson

flutter of prayer flags—

the Dalai Lama laughing

at his own joke

Judt Shrode

lost in joy

the tranquil Buddha

on our bookshelf

Bill Waters

the teakettle sings

we achieve

enlightenment

Richard Magahiz

newborn . . .

one hand on earth

the other in heaven

Ron C. Moss

a snowy path . . .

candles lead to

Buddha

Corine Timmer

February 28

nature (pure nature)

thorny quince in bloom—
a birdcall pierces
the morning

— Judt Shrode

morning walk . . .
all the water reeds
lean to one side

    Jayashree Maniyil

passing shower . . .
the warming turtles backtrack
into cool

    Pris Campbell

South breeze

swaying banana leaves

reflect the moon

Ajaya Mahala

shallow pond . . .

blue heron

in deep focus

Corine Timmer

snowmelt . . .

the river brimming

with clouds

Pamela Cooper

starlight

in the tree rings

mouse droppings

    Michael Dylan Welch

endless afternoon . . .

a copperhead swims

across the lake

    John Hawk

sultry sun

a last dragon cloud

wisps away

    Hansha Teki

thorny quince in bloom—

a birdcall pierces

the morning

    Judt Shrode

NEXT STEPS WITH HAIKU

HAIKU IS A WAY OF SHARING MOMENTS of personal experience with another person. In Japan, where this poetry originated, traditional haiku uses a pattern of five, seven, and then five sounds (not to be confused with syllables) in a single vertical line. A three-line presentation is most common in English, with a growing practice of using one line to more closely approximate the Japanese form. Variations include visual or concrete haiku, vertical alignments, or other creative variations, which may all work well if the poem's content remains primarily experiential in sharing a keenly perceived everyday moment. In English, ten to fourteen syllables is about the same length as the seventeen sounds in Japanese. In both languages, a traditional haiku employs a *kigo* or season word, telling readers when the poem is taking place. It also uses a *kireji* or cutting word to divide the poem into two parts. In English, this effect is created by giving the poem two grammatically separate parts (never three). The "cut" between the two juxtaposed parts is sometimes indicated with punctuation, often a dash or ellipsis. Even without punctuation, however, you should be able to observe a cut or pause in the grammar between the first and second parts of the poem, together with a shift of images. Haiku (the word is both singular and plural) dwell chiefly in objective images, minimizing any subjective commentary or analysis. They also use the five senses and present tense to help make the poem's experience immediate and personal. Each poem should offer you something that you can taste, touch, smell, see, or hear—and also feel emotionally. A good haiku makes the ordinary extraordinary by offering its close attention, and as a reader your continued close attention "finishes" the poem.

Haiku do not have titles, and nearly always avoid rhyme, as well as overt metaphor and simile, but they can take advantage of assonance, consonance, and other poetic techniques to help make the poem lyrical and engaging. It has been said that haiku is like a finger pointing to the moon, and if the finger is bejeweled, we no longer see the moon. Certain poetic techniques are best kept to a minimum, seeming almost invisible, as if the words themselves vanish in place of meaning, implication, and emotional effect.

It is possible to write haiku about nearly anything—they need not be limited just to the beautiful. Indeed, haiku can be dark or light in their subject matter and tone. But regardless of the feelings they evoke, the best of these poems often celebrate ordinary, everyday experiences—Jack Kerouac said that haiku should be as simple as porridge. A haiku paints a clear and sharply focused picture for others to relate to in sensory and emotional ways.

This poetry has a rich tradition in Japanese, stretching back many centuries. Haiku in English began adding its own traditions more than a hundred years ago, and now haiku is written in many languages around the world. While haiku is often mistaught as being merely anything in a pattern of five-seven-five syllables, it's worth moving beyond popular beliefs that are often oversimplified and even misguided to discover the more challenging disciplines—and rewards—of this poetic art.

To learn more about English-language haiku, it is useful to read some of its foremost books, such as William J. Higginson's *The Haiku Handbook*, Cor van den Heuvel's *The Haiku Anthology*, and Jim Kacian's *Haiku in English: The First Hundred Years*. Translations of the leading Japanese masters are also recommended, especially those featuring Bashō, Buson, Issa, Shiki, and Chiyo-ni. Good books to start with are Robert Hass's *The Essential Haiku*, and translations by Stephen Addiss, Haruo Shirane, and Makoto Ueda, among others. The older translations of R. H. Blyth and Harold G. Henderson have much to offer as well. But do not dwell only in the past or presume that haiku is just what was written hundreds of years ago, or think of it as a "Zen" art, which is how it is sometimes taught in the West. Instead, look for translations by recent and contemporary Japanese haiku poets as well, where you'll discover a variety of approaches that typically have nothing to do with Zen. Haiku continues to be a living art in Japan.

Children also deserve good information. An excellent book for introducing children to writing and appreciating haiku is Patricia Donegan's *Haiku: Asian Arts and Crafts for Creative Kids*. Be wary of lesson plans online that believe they have taught haiku successfully by telling students simply to count syllables.

Organizations such as the Haiku Society of America, Haiku Canada, the British Haiku Society, the Yuki Teikei Haiku Society, and Japan's Haiku International Association are well worth joining to benefit from their meetings and news, and especially their journals, such as *Frogpond*, *Haiku Canada Review*, *Blithe Spirit*, and *Geppo*. Other journals worth reading are *Modern Haiku*, *The Heron's Nest*, *Acorn*, *Hummingbird*, *Mayfly*, *Bottle Rockets*, and *Presence*, among many others, both in print and online.

You might also enjoy Haiku North America, the world's largest haiku conference outside Japan, held every two years since 1991, which has served to be the haiku community's most significant and inspirational gathering of the tribes. Smaller regional haiku retreats also take place annually in various locations, such as the Seabeck Haiku Getaway that I direct. In California, the American Haiku Archives preserves the world's largest collection of haiku materials outside Japan, including books, journals, and ephemera. And be sure to look for local haiku groups that might meet near where you live. You can find these groups by networking with people who lead national organizations or by searching online.

The Haiku Foundation is perhaps the leading online repository for information about haiku in English. It offers discussion forums, featured poems, news and announcements, digital archives, lists of journal and contest submission deadlines, resources for teaching haiku, and a directory of haiku poets. The Haiku Society of America website also provides extensive information about haiku, as well as winners from its many contests for haiku, senryu, and related poetry. A map of the society's various regional groups makes it easy to connect. The website for *Modern Haiku* magazine presents numerous essays and reviews from its past issues. Many personal websites and blogs feature haiku, senryu, and commentary, often with great enthusiasm, but some of these sites are unreliable sources of haiku information.

Social media also offers much opportunity for haiku sharing and feedback, such as the NaHaiWriMo page on Facebook, which encourages the daily writing of haiku—with writing prompts provided year-round, not just in the official month of February. Searches for haiku on Instagram, Pinterest, YouTube, Twitter, Tumblr, Google Plus, and even LinkedIn reveal much to explore, but with the usual caveats about popular misperceptions.

Small presses that specialize in haiku include Alba Publishing, Bottle Rockets Press, Brooks Books, Press Here, Red Moon Press, and Snapshot Press, among others, all of which are well worth seeking out, especially the annual Red Moon anthologies.

Many organizations also have haiku contests that you might consider entering. Some charge a fee, which helps to support the organization, but you can also find a number of free English-language haiku contests around the world.

Haiku is widely mistaught in Western schools and textbooks simply as a syllable-counting exercise. Writing haiku with a five-seven-five syllable pattern is where many people start, which is always a choice that anyone is free to make, but haiku offers many rewards and challenges beyond painting by numbers. Above all, your pursuit of haiku should remain enjoyable.

You might also be interested in related genres of poetry, such as senryu (a more humorous or satirical variation of haiku), tanka (a much older genre of poetry than haiku, written in five lines in English), haibun (chiefly autobiographical prose with haiku interspersed or at the end), haiga (paintings with haiku added in calligraphy), shahai, or photo-haiga (photographs with typeset haiku), and linked-verse forms such as renku, renga, tan-renga, and rengay. I explore many of these forms on my personal website, Graceguts.com, which also offers numerous essays and reviews relating to the learning and appreciation of haiku poetry.

The way of haiku is never-ending. It is indeed a hand beckoning, a door half-opened, a mirror wiped clean. May your next steps with haiku include NaHaiWriMo, and much more, as you continue to share in the daily celebration of this inspiring poetry.

Contributing Poets

Apanius, Dawn / Hudson, Ohio. 70, 75, 80, 145
Ashbaugh, Marilyn / Edwardsburg, Michigan 99
Asopa, Sanjuktaa / Belgaum, India. 67, 72, 93, 99, 109, 179
Baranski, Johnny / Vancouver, Washington. 34, 43, 85, 102, 114, 193, 207, 211, 218
Bellini, Marina / Mantua, Italy. 64, 141, 145, 159
Bilbro, Peggy Hale / Huntsville, Alabama. 48, 97, 102
Bjerg, Johannes S. H. / Højby, Denmark. 56, 84
Broughton, Belinda / Adelaide, Australia 25
Buffington, Susan E. / New Hartford, New York 16, 69, 219
Burgevin, Anne / State College, Pennsylvania. 14
Campbell, Pris / Lake Worth, Florida. 99, 106, 159, 191, 196, 226
Connolly, Joseph / Tinian, Northern Mariana Islands 187, 209
Cooper, Pamela / Montréal, Québec 84, 129, 143, 195, 227
Cox, Gillena / Port of Spain, Trinidad and Tobago 50
Deavers, Marilyn / Windsor Heights, Iowa 44
Decker, Karla / Lincoln, Nebraska 37, 173, 193
DeLorean, Anne Larbes / West Chester, Ohio 122, 204
Dickson, Scott / Temple, Texas 219
Duffy, Mike / Seattle, Washington 55, 142, 156, 216
Franson, Robert T. / Santa Cruz, California 42, 143, 200
Freilinger, Ida / Redmond, Washington 92
French, Terri L. / Huntsville, Alabama 26, 42, 85, 201, 217
Galton, Grace / East Huntspill, United Kingdom 68, 131, 174, 194
Ghose, Samar / Perth, Australia 30, 36, 44, 69, 132
Green, Rachel / Chesterfield, United Kingdom 38

Hardin, Patty / Long Beach, Washington. 43
Harrison, Devin / Duncan, British Columbia 115, 218
Harter, Penny / Mays Landing, New Jersey. 86, 98, 115, 122
Harvey, Michele L. / Hamilton, New York. 24, 69, 78, 107, 172, 180, 195, 203, 217
Hawk, John / Columbus, Ohio. 16, 46, 70, 91, 93, 120, 144, 158, 179, 192, 209, 218, 228
Herman, Randall / Concord, Nebraska. 114, 180
Hoarau, Vincent / Lyon, France. 18
Huppen, Iocasta / Brussels, Belgium 48, 70, 132, 217
Jäderberg, Helene / Gothenburg, Sweden 26, 78, 86, 105, 109, 203, 210
James, Maggie 108, 157
Jolyot, Line / Nantes, France. 55, 128
Kaufmann, Barbara / Massapequa Park, New York. 29, 37, 45, 56, 120
Kendall, Mary / Chapel Hill, North Carolina. 108
Kindelberger, Roy / Bothell, Washington 123, 180
Kingston, Robert / Rayleigh, United Kingdom 33, 38, 62, 85, 100, 172, 193, 204
Kolodji, Deborah P / Temple City, California 24, 35
Krause, Shelley / Princeton, New Jersey. 18, 55, 71, 92, 121, 150, 174
Krishnamurthy, Shrikaanth / Birmingham, United Kingdom. 17, 172, 202
Laier, Vibeke / Randers, Denmark 68
Lee, Michael Henry / Saint Augustine, Florida. 37, 54, 78, 131, 156, 166
Lohman, Eric / Powder Springs, Georgia 71, 196
Longenecker, Greg / Pasadena, California 14

Losak, Amy / Teaneck, New Jersey 43
MacRury, Carole / Point Roberts, Washington 34, 45, 53, 57, 63, 114, 123, 130
Magahiz, Richard / San Mateo, California 220
Mahala, Ajaya / Pune, India 49, 127, 132, 145, 196, 227
Maire, Marie-Alice / Rungis, France 76
Maniyil, Jayashree / Melbourne, Australia 201, 226
Marinova, Viktoriya / Pleven City, Bulgaria 27
McGregor, Marietta / Canberra, Australia 29
McGregor, Rowena / Ipswich, Australia 77
Mena, Paul David / Wayland, Massachusetts 19, 35, 46, 79, 100, 113, 116, 144, 181, 200, 210
Moore, Michael A. / DeSoto, Texas 83, 87, 130
Moss, Ron C. / Leslie Vale, Australia 49, 54, 63, 122, 187, 211, 221
Mount, Cameron / Galloway, New Jersey 27, 45, 57, 151, 161, 194
Murata, Susan / Swanzey, New Hampshire 128
Nelson, Pat / Bethlehem, Pennsylvania 101, 187
Nguyen, Kathy Uyen / Houston, Texas 28, 123, 157, 179, 119
Nissen-Wade, Rosemary / Murwillumbah, Australia 50, 71, 173
Nonk, Nink / Semarang, Indonesia 160
Olson, Erica / Plains, Montana 17, 144
Papanicolaou, Linda / Stanford, California 27, 49, 106
Paterson, Joanna 29
Penchev, Nikolay / Sofia, Bulgaria 13, 19, 100, 157
Pierides, Stella / Neusäß, Germany 23, 30, 115, 173
Popescu, Virginia / Ploiesti, Romania 167
Pottier, Nicole / Évreux, France 201
Pray, Sandi / Robbinsville, North Carolina 25, 77, 136
Ray, Ardelle / Las Vegas, Nevada 101, 129, 137
Renn, Symanntha / Diamond, Missouri 137

Rodriguez, James / Washougal, Washington. 18
Sangotte, Rahmatou / Paris, France. 17, 107, 155, 161
Shepherd, Deborah B. / Midland, Virginia. 107
Shrode, Judt / Tacoma, Washington. 220, 225, 229
Skanne, Caroline / Upnor, United Kingdom 25
Smolak, Steve / Murphysboro, Illinois 178, 208
Sterba, Carmen / University Place, Washington 47, 131, 150
Strang, Barbara / Christchurch, New Zealand 15, 54, 76, 166, 177, 181, 186
Sverredal, Tore / Göteborg, Sweden 15, 35, 44, 80, 109
Taleb, Allal / Dilbeek, Belgium. 143
Teki, Hansha / Paraparaumu, New Zealand 116, 142, 229
Timmer, Corine / Faro, Portugal 116, 215, 221, 227
Turner, Patsy / Akaroa, New Zealand. 151, 160, 199, 204
Varma, Anitha / Kochi, India 36, 77, 137, 159, 194
Villa, Christine L. / Sacramento, California . . . 28, 61, 64, 98, 186, 209
Waters, Bill / Pennington, New Jersey 79, 92, 130, 171, 174, 220
Welch, Michael Dylan / Sammamish, Washington 15, 46, 56, 63, 79, 93, 121, 136, 158, 167, 188, 195, 210, 228
Werren, Angie / Amelia, Ohio. 24, 87, 121
Williams, Alison / Southampton, United Kingdom . . . 30, 150, 208, 216
Wilson, Kathabela / Pasadena, California. 80, 136, 149, 151
Windsor, Sheila / Bexhill, United Kingdom. 36, 41, 50, 57, 72, 108, 129, 192
Winteridge, Sara (Eider Green) /
    Fordingbridge, United Kingdom 26, 87, 185, 188, 192, 203
Wright, Kathi / Grants Pass, Oregon 165, 167, 202
Wruck, Paul / Strasburg, Pennsylvania. 47, 62, 178
Yaninska, Gergana / Plovdiv, Bulgaria. 16, 86

www.ingramcontent.com/pod-product-compliance
Lightning Source LLC
Chambersburg PA
CBHW062200080426
42734CB00010B/1754